The Declaration of Independence

Edited and Introduced
by
Wim Coleman

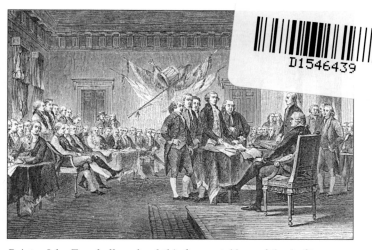

*Painter John Trumbull rendered this famous tableau of the drafting com-
mittee presenting its declaration to the Continental Congress. Jefferson
himself advised him about details of the scene. Trumbull went to great
pains to portray the participants accurately and at their appropriate ages.
But after Trumbull's work was completed, he was upset to learn that
Jefferson's architectural details were incorrect. (Library of Congress)*

Discovery Enterprises, Ltd.
Carlisle, Massachusetts

© Discovery Enterprises, Ltd., Carlisle, MA 1997

ISBN 1-57960-024-7 paperback edition
Library of Congress Catalog Card Number 97-68485

10   9   8   7   6   5   4   3   2   1

Printed in the United States of America

Subject Reference Guide:

The Declaration of Independence
edited and introduced by Wim Coleman

The Declaration of Independence — U. S. History

Thomas Jefferson — U. S. History

Thomas Paine's *Common Sense* — U. S. History

Photo Credits:

Cover illustration: The first public reading of the
Declaration of Independence
(*Harper's Weekly*, July 15, 1876, by Edwin A. Abbey)

Illustrations courtesy of Dover Publications, Inc., New York;
except p. 26, from *Pictorial History of American Presidents*,
A.S. Barnes and Company, New York

Editor's photo by John Nance

Editor's notes regarding the documents:
1. *All original spelling has been retained.*
2. *A full line of dots indicates the deletion of at least an entire paragraph.*

Table of Contents

Introduction:
As Independence Approaches

by
Wim Coleman

Washington Irving's immortal character Rip Van Winkle slept right through the arrival of American independence. As generations of school children have learned, Rip fell into a deep, twenty-year sleep in the wilds of the Catskills after drinking from a mysterious flagon. When he returned to his village, he found that everything had changed — including the political situation, as the following selection indicates.

Source: Washington Irving, *The Complete Tales of Washington Irving*, ed. Charles Neider, Garden City: Doubleday, 1975, pp. 10-11.

He now hurried forth, and hastened to his old resort, the village inn, but it too was gone. A large rickety wooden building stood in its place with great gaping windows, some of them broken and mended with old hats and petticoats, and over the door was painted, "The Union Hotel, by Jonathan Doolittle." Instead of the great tree that used to shelter the quiet little Dutch inn of yore, there now was reared a tall naked pole, with something on top that looked like a red night-cap, and from it was fluttering a flag, on which was a singular assemblage of stars and stripes; — all this was strange and incomprehensible. He recognized on the sign, however, the ruby face of King George, under which he had smoked so many a peaceful pipe; but even this was singularly metamorphosed. The red coat was changed for one of blue and buff, a sword was held in the hand instead of a sceptre, the head was decorated with a cocked hat, and underneath was painted in large characters, GENERAL WASHINGTON....

The appearance of Rip, with his long, grizzled beard, his rusty fowling-piece, his uncouth dress, and an army of women and children at his heels, soon attracted the attention of the tavern-politicians. They crowded around him, eying him from head to foot with great curiosity. The orator bustled up to him, and, drawing him partly aside, inquired "On which side he voted?" Rip stared in vacant stupidity. Another short but busy little fellow pulled him by the arm, and, rising on tiptoe, inquired in his ear, "Whether he was Federal or Democrat?" Rip was equally at a loss to comprehend the question; when a knowing, self-important old gentleman, in a sharp cocked hat, made his way through the crowd, putting them to the right and left with his elbows as he passed, and planting himself before Van Winkle, with one arm akimbo, the other resting on his cane, his keen eyes and sharp hat penetrating, as it were, into his very soul, demanded in an austere tone, "What brought him to the election with a gun on his shoulder, and a mob at his heels; and whether he meant to breed a riot in the village?" — "Alas! gentlemen," cried Rip, somewhat dismayed, "I am a poor quiet man, a native of the place, and a loyal subject of the King, God bless him!"

Here a general shout burst from the by-standers — "A tory! a tory! a spy! a refugee! hustle him! away with him!"

Perhaps we find it too easy to laugh at the confusion of a simple underachiever like Rip Van Winkle. Would any of his more accomplished contemporaries have been less confused in his situation? What about the men who voted for the adoption of the Declaration of Independence? What if any one of them had fallen asleep before the outbreak of the Revolutionary War, not to awaken for twenty years?

Few if any of them would have been less perplexed upon awakening than Rip himself — and by far the greater number would have uttered a similar plea of loyalty to the king. Before 1775, virtually nobody imagined the possibility of American independence. But in July of

1776, the British colonies declared themselves a new, sovereign nation. What happened to change the course of American history so abruptly and so fatefully?

Jamestown, the first permanent English settlement in America, was founded in 1607, and for about a century and a half after that, British Americans considered themselves loyal subjects of the mother country. By various charters and agreements, thirteen British colonies were founded along the Atlantic seaboard. In theory, the British could exploit these colonies much as they pleased. But in practice, the British essentially left the colonies alone. True, they imposed a few modest taxes to regulate trade. But these were easily evaded by the colonists, for whom the practice of smuggling was considered an honorable profession, praised by as distinguished a citizen as John Adams of Massachusetts. Great Britain was an indulgent parent; she and her North American colonies coexisted in mutual affection and respect.

Arguably, the high point of this relationship was the French and Indian War (1754-1763). When France tried to take control of North America, Britons and colonists fought side by side against a common foe. Unfortunately, after the British-Colonial victory, Great Britain found herself deeply in debt. To pay off this debt, the British at last saw fit to exploit the colonies in earnest. And the colonists were not happy about it.

They had, after all, become used to self-rule, which they considered their right as British subjects. The colonies elected their own assemblies, passed their own laws, issued their own money, and collected their own taxes. Not surprisingly, they resented it when Britain decided to maintain a standing army in America. Moreover, the British demanded that the colonies contribute to this army's support; colonists were even forced to quarter soldiers in their own homes. Colonial resentment grew when Britain forbade settlement anywhere west of the Allegheny Mountains. The British also denied colonial assemblies the right to issue their own money and imposed tougher import duties on such goods as molasses. A greater shock came when the British imposed the Stamp Act upon the colonies in 1765.

This act was intended to impose a tax on such items on newspapers, playing cards, dice, and legal documents. The colonists would have none of it. They convened the Stamp Act Congress, which established an effective boycott against the act, causing it to be repealed in 1766. But the bitterness created by this measure never really disappeared, and Great Britain continued trying to impose her will upon the colonists. The Townshend Acts created further import duties, and the New York Assembly was suspended for its refusal to agree to the quartering of troops. Toward the end of the 1760s, the British began to send more and more troops to America in hopes of bringing her unruly colonists back into line.

Boston, Massachusetts became a hotbed of resistance against the British. In 1770, five colonists were shot and killed by British soldiers when a mob attacked the Boston Customs House; this became known as the Boston Massacre.

Paul Revere's engraving of the Boston Massacre.

In 1773, the British tried to coerce the colonists into purchasing tea from the British East India Company and paying a stiff duty for it. On December 16 of that year, a mysterious gang of Bostonians disguised themselves as Indians and committed one of the most ambitious and destructive acts of vandalism in human history, dumping tons of unsold British tea into the Boston harbor. This became known as the Boston Tea Party.

The British responded to the Boston Tea Party by blockading Boston. This stringent punishment aroused the sympathy of the American colonies, who convened the Continental Congress in 1774. Congress organized an effective boycott and sent petitions to Great Britain. Its members were determined to restore what they believed to be their natural rights as British subjects; they had no notion of declaring independence from the mother country. The First Continental Congress adjourned on October 26, 1774, with plans to reconvene on May 10, 1775.

Then, early in 1775, King George III and the British Parliament decided to use military force to subdue the colonists. Troops were sent to Concord, Massachusetts to destroy military supplies there. On April 19, those troops were met in Lexington by a band of armed colonists. Shots were fired and lives were lost, first in Lexington and then at Concord.

The Revolutionary War had begun. While Rip Van Winkle lay asleep in the Catskills, his America was changing forever. A little less than a year after the battles of Lexington and Concord, the unimaginable would happen. Independence from Britain would become a reality. And Congress' Declaration of Independence would justify that decision in memorable and powerful language which resounds to the present day.

The Historical Moment

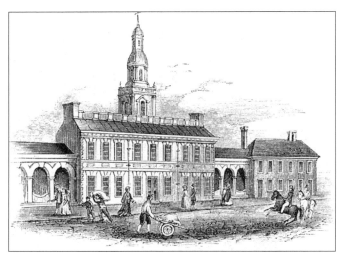

An engraving of the Philadelphia State House, later known as Independence Hall. It was here that the Second Continental Congress met and adopted the Declaration of Independence.

On May 10, 1775, the Second Continental Congress convened at the Philadelphia State House, later known as Independence Hall. The battles at Lexington and Concord had taken place just three weeks before. As one of their first items of business, the delegates had to make a formal declaration of war. Although few of them realized it yet, they were headed inexorably down the road toward independence from Britain.

The Declaration of Causes for Taking Up Arms

On July 6, 1775, Congress issued the Declaration of the Causes for Taking Up Arms, drafted in part by Virginia's Thomas Jefferson and Pennsylvania's John Dickinson. Here is the opening paragraph of this document.

Source: Thomas Jefferson, *The Papers of Thomas Jefferson*, vol. 1, ed. Julian P. Boyd, Princeton: Princeton University Press, 1950, pp. 213-4.

If it was possible for Men, who exercise their Reason to believe, that the Divine Author of our Existence intended a part of the human Race to hold an absolute Property in, and an unbounded Power of others, marked out by his infinite Goodness and Wisdom, as the Objects of a legal Domination never rightfully resistible, however severe and oppressive, the Inhabitants of these Colonies might at least require from the Parliament of Great-Britain some Evidence, that this dreadful Authority over them has been granted to that Body. But a Reverence for our great Creator, Principles of Humanity, and the Dictates of Common Sense, must convince all those who reflect upon the Subject, that Government was instituted to promote the Welfare of Mankind, and ought to be administered for the Attainment of that End. The Legislature of Great-Britain, however, stimulated by an inordinate Passion for a Power not only unjustifiable, but which they know to be peculiarly reprobated by the very Constitution of that Kingdom, and desperate of Success in any Mode of Contest, where Regard should be had to Truth, Law, or Right, have at Length, deserting those, attempted to effect their cruel and impolitic Purpose of enslaving these Colonies by Violence, and have thereby *rendered it necessary for us to close with their last Appeal from Reason to Arms.* Yet, however blinded that Assembly may be, by their intemperate Rage for unlimited Domination, so to Slight Justice and the Opinion of Mankind, we esteem ourselves bound by Obligations of Respect to the Rest of the World, to make known the Justice of our cause.

Most of the document was devoted to past grievances against Great Britain, culminating in the attacks on Lexington and Concord. The closing paragraphs of the Declaration follow. Note that Congress diplomatically insisted that the colonies were not seeking independence — "not yet."

Source: Thomas Jefferson, *op. cit.*, pp. 217-8.

In brief, a part of these Colonies now feel, and all of them are sure of feeling, as far as the Vengeance of Administration can inflict them, the complicated Calamities of Fire, Sword, and Famine. We are reduced to the alternative of chusing an unconditional Submission to the tyranny of irritated Ministers, or resistance by Force. The latter is our choice. We have counted the cost of this contest, and find nothing so dreadful as voluntary Slavery. Honour, Justice, and Humanity, forbid us tamely to surrender that Freedom which we received from our gallant Ancestors, and which our innocent Posterity have a right to receive from us. We cannot endure the infamy and guilt of resigning succeeding Generations to that wretchedness which inevitably awaits them, if we basely entail hereditary Bondage upon them.

Our cause is just. Our union is perfect. Our internal Resources are great, and, if necessary, foreign Assistance is undoubtedly attainable. We gratefully acknowledge, as signal Instances of the Divine Favour towards us, that his Providence would not permit us to be called into this severe Controversy, until we were grown up to our present strength, had been previously exercised in warlike Operation, and possessed of the means of defending ourselves. With hearts fortified with these animating Reflections, *we most solemnly, before God and the World, declare, that, exerting the utmost Energy of those Powers, which our beneficent Creator hath graciously bestowed upon us, the Arms we have been compelled by our Enemies to assume, we will, in defiance of every Hazard, with unabating Firmness and Perseverence, employ for the preservation of our Liberties;* being with one Mind resolved to die Freemen rather than to live Slaves.

Lest this Declaration should disquiet the Minds of our Friends and Fellow-Subjects in any part of the Empire, we assure them that we mean not to dissolve that Union which has so long and so happily subsisted between us, and which we sincerely wish to see restored. Necessity has not yet driven us into that desperate Measure, or induced us to excite any other Nation to War against them. We have not raised Armies with ambitious Designs of separating from Great-Britain, and establishing Independent States. *We fight not for Glory or for Conquest. We exhibit to Mankind the remarkable Spectacle of a People attacked by unprovoked Enemies, without any imputation or even suspicion of Offence.* They boast of their Privileges and Civilization, and yet proffer no milder Conditions than Servitude or Death.

In our own native Land, in defence of the Freedom that is our Birthright, and which we ever enjoyed till the late Violation of it — for the protection of our Property, acquired solely by the honest Industry of our fore-fathers and ourselves, *against Violence actually offered, we have taken up Arms. We shall lay them down when Hostilities shall cease on the part of the Aggressors, and all danger of their being renewed shall be removed, and not before.*

With an humble Confidence in the Mercies of the supreme and impartial Judge and Ruler of the Universe, *we most devoutly implore his Divine Goodness to protect us happily through this great Conflict, to dispose our Adversaries to reconciliation on reasonable Terms, and thereby to relieve the Empire from the Calamities of civil War.*

Revolution by Natural Law

Even the more moderate delegates to Congress did not regard resistance to Britain as a radical measure. They had the precedent of the Glorious Revolution on their side — the revolution which, during the 1680s, deposed James II, making William of Orange and his wife Mary king and queen. The sixteenth-century philosopher John Locke justified this revolution by natural law.

According to Locke's theory, mankind was born into a "state of nature" — a world without government. Man gave up this blissful but precarious state by his own consent, as Locke explained in the following passage from his Second Treatise of Government.

Source: John Locke, *Second Treatise of Government*, Ed, Richard H. Cox, Arlington Heights, Illinois: Harlan Davidson, 1982, p. 75.

If man in the state of nature be so free, as has been said; if he be absolute lord of his own person and possessions, equal to the greatest, and subject to no body, why will he part with his freedom? Why will he give up this empire, and subject himself to the dominion and control of any other power? To which 'tis obvious to answer, that though in the state of nature he hath such a right, yet the enjoyment of it is very uncertain and constantly exposed to the invasion of others. For all being kings as much as he, every man is equal, and the greater part no strict observers of equity and justice, the enjoyment of the property he has in this state is very unsafe, very unsecure. This makes him willing to quit a condition, which however free, is full of fears and continual dangers: and 'tis not without reason, that he seeks out, and is willing to join in society with others who are already united, or have a mind to unite for the mutual preservation of their lives, liberties, and estates, which I call by the general name, property.

According to this idea, it was obvious to Locke that no government had the right to rule without the consent of the governed, as he explained in the following passage.

Source: John Locke, *op. cit.*, p. 135.

The reason why men enter into society, is the preservation of their property; and the end why they choose and authorize a legislative, is, that there may be laws made, and rules set as guards and fences to the properties of all the members of the society, to limit the power, and moderate the dominion of every part and member of the society. For since it can never be supposed to be the will of the society, that the legislative should have a power to destroy that, which every one designs to secure by entering into society, and for which the people submitted themselves to the legislators of their own making; whenever the *legislators endeavour to take away, and destroy the property of the people*, or to reduce them to slavery under arbitrary power, they put themselves into a state of war with the people, who are thereupon absolved from any farther obedience, and are left to the common refuge, which God hath provided for all men, against force and violence. Whensoever therefore the *legislative* shall transgress this fundamental rule of society; and either by ambition, fear, folly, or corruption, *endeavour to grasp* themselves, *or put into the hands of any other an absolute power* over the lives, liberties, and estates of the people; by this breach of trust they *forfeit the power*, the people had put into their hands, for quite contrary ends, and it devolves to the people, who have a right to resume their original liberty, and by the establishment of a new legislative (such as they shall think fit) provide for their own safety and security, which is the end for which they are in society.

Locke made clear the right of people to rebel against a tyrant — by force, if necessary.

Source: John Locke, *op. cit.*, pp. 140-1.

The end of government is the good of mankind, and which is *best for mankind*, that the people should be always exposed to the boundless will of tyranny, or that the rulers should be sometimes liable to be opposed, when they grow exorbitant in the use of their power, and employ it for the destruction, and not the preservation of the properties of their people?...

This I am sure, whoever, either ruler or subject, by force goes about to invade the rights of either prince or people, and lays the foundation for *overturning* the constitution and frame of *any just government*, is guilty of the greatest crime, I think, a man is capable of, being to answer for all those mischiefs of blood, rapine, and desolation, which the breaking to pieces of governments bring on a country, and he who does it, is justly to be esteemed the common enemy and pest of mankind; and is to be treated accordingly.

Thomas Paine's **Common Sense**

Thomas Paine

On January 10, 1776, while Congress struggled to decide the future of the colonies, a small book appeared which swayed the debate toward independence. This was Common Sense, *written by Thomas Paine, an English political activist living in America. It had tremendous popular appeal, quickly selling more than 100,000 copies.*

16

Paine's argument was startling and very radical. In the passage below, he attacked the whole principle of monarchy — a dangerous viewpoint at a time when many people still believed that kings ruled by divine right. But as radical as Paine was, a great many colonists found that they agreed with him.

Source: Thomas Paine, *Rights of Man, Common Sense, and Other Political Writings*, ed. Mark Philp, Oxford: Oxford University Press, 1995, pp. 17-19.

But it is not so much the absurdity as the evil of hereditary succession which concerns mankind. Did it ensure a race of good and wise men it would have the seal of divine authority, but as it opens a door to the *foolish*, the *wicked*, and the *improper*, it hath in it the nature of oppression. Men who look upon themselves born to reign, and others to obey, soon grow insolent; selected from the rest of mankind their minds are early poisoned by importance; and the world they act in differs so materially from the world at large, that they have but little opportunity of knowing its true interests, and when they succeed to the government are frequently the most ignorant and unfit of any throughout the dominions.

Another evil which attends hereditary succession is, that the throne is subject to be possessed by a minor at any age; all which time the regency, acting under the cover of a king, have every opportunity and inducement to betray their trust. The same national misfortune happens, when a king worn out with age and infirmity, enters the last stage of human weakness. In both these cases the public becomes a prey to every miscreant, who can tamper successfully with the follies either of age or infancy.

The most plausible plea, which hath ever been offered in favour of hereditary succession, is, that it preserves a nation from civil wars; and were this true, it would be weighty; whereas, it is the most barefaced falsity ever imposed upon mankind. The whole history of England disowns the fact. Thirty kings and two minors have reigned in that distracted kingdom since the conquest, in which time there have been

17

(including the Revolution)[1] no less than eight civil wars and nineteen rebellions. Wherefore instead of making for peace, it makes against it, and destroys the very foundation it seems to stand on....

In short, monarchy and succession have laid (not this or that kingdom only) but the world in blood and ashes. 'Tis a form of government which the word of God bears testimony against, and blood will attend it....

In England a king hath little more to do than to make war and give away places; which in plain terms is to impoverish the nation and set it together by the ears. A pretty business indeed for a man to be allowed eight hundred thousand sterling a year for, and worshipped into the bargain! Of more worth is one honest man to society, and in the sight of God, than all the crowned ruffians that ever lived.

England might be a constitutional monarchy with an elected parliament, but (argued Paine) it was still a monarchy and therefore scarcely able to govern itself, let alone the inhabitants of a huge continent on the other side of an ocean. Paine's rhetoric reached a fevered pitch as he pleaded for America's separation from England.

Source: Thomas Paine, *op. cit.*, p. 35.

Ye that tell us of harmony and reconciliation, can ye restore to us the time that is past? Can ye give to prostitution its former innocence? Neither can ye reconcile Britain and America. The last cord now is broken, the people of England are presenting addresses against us. There are injuries which nature cannot forgive; she would cease to be nature if she did. As well can the lover forgive the ravisher of his mistress, as the continent forgive the murders of Britain. The Almighty hath implanted

[1] i.e., England's Glorious Revolution of 1688-89.

18

in us these unextinguishable feelings for good and wise purposes. They are the guardians of his image in our hearts. They distinguish us from the herd of common animals. The social compact would dissolve, and justice be extirpated the earth, or have only a casual existence were we callous to the touches of affection. The robber and the murderer, would often escape unpunished, did not the injuries which our tempers sustain, provoke us into justice.

O ye that love mankind! Ye that dare oppose, not only the tyranny, but the tyrant, stand forth! Every spot of the old world is over-run with oppression. Freedom hath been hunted round the globe. Asia, and Africa, have long expelled her. — Europe regards her like a stranger, and England hath given her warning to depart. O! receive the fugitive, and prepare an asylum for mankind.

Paine closed his book on a more rational note, insisting that the time had come for a formal Declaration of Independence from Great Britain.

Source: Thomas Paine, *op. cit*. pp. 45-6.

TO CONCLUDE, however strange it may appear to some, or however unwilling they may be to think so, matters not, but many strong and striking reasons may be given, to shew, that nothing can settle our affairs so expeditiously as an open and determined declaration for independance. Some of which are,

First. — It is the custom of nations, when any two are at war, for some other powers, not engaged in the quarrel, to step in as mediators, and bring about the preliminaries of a peace: but while America calls herself the subject of Great Britain, no power, however well disposed she may be, can offer her mediation. Wherefore, in our present state, we may quarrel on forever.

Secondly. — It is unreasonable to suppose, that France or Spain will give us any kind of assistance, if we mean only to make use of that assistance for the purpose of repairing the breach, and strengthening the connection between Britain and America, because, those powers would be sufferers by the consequences.

Thirdly. — While we profess ourselves the subjects of Britain, we must, in the eye of foreign nations, be considered as rebels. The precedent is somewhat dangerous to *their peace*, for men to be in arms under the name of subjects; we on the spot, can solve the paradox: but to unite resistance and subjection, requires an idea much too refined for common understanding.

Fourthly. — Were a manifesto to be published, and despatched to foreign courts, setting forth the miseries we have endured, and the peaceable methods we have ineffectually used for redress; declaring, at the same time, that not being able, any longer to live happily or safely upon the cruel disposition of the British court, we had been driven to the necessity of breaking off all connection with her; at the same time assuring all such courts of our peaceable disposition towards them, and of our desire of entering into trade with them: Such a memorial would produce more good effects to this Continent, than if a ship were freighted with petitions to Britain.

Under our present denomination of British subjects we can neither be received nor heard abroad: The custom of all courts is against us, and will be so, until, by an independance, we take rank with other nations.

These proceedings may at first appear strange and difficult; but, like all other steps which we have already passed over, will in a little time become familiar and agreeable; and, until an independance is declared, the Continent will feel itself like a man who continues putting off some unpleasant business from day to day, yet knows it must be done, hates to set about it, wishes it over, and is continually haunted with the thoughts of its necessity.

Hopes for an American Republic

Paine's Common Sense *helped force the issue of independence in the colonies. In May 1776, the Massachusetts House of Representatives advised towns in the colony to begin debating the matter of independence. The following selection is from a resolution approved by a town meeting in Malden, Massachusetts and sent to Congress.*

Source: William Dudley, ed., *The American Revolution: Opposing Viewpoints®*, San Diego: Greenhaven Press, 1992, pp. 128-9. (Citation by Dudley: Hezekiah Niles, ed., Principles and Acts of the Revolution in America, Baltimore, 1822.)

SIR — A resolution of the hon. house of representatives, calling upon the several towns in this colony to express their minds with respect to the important question of American independence, is the occasion of our now instructing you. The time was, sir, when we loved the king and the people of Great Britain with an affection truly filial; we felt ourselves interested in their glory; we shared in their joys and sorrows; we cheerfully poured the fruit of all our labours into the lap of our mother country, and without reluctance expended our blood and our treasure in their cause.

These were our sentiments toward Great Britain while she continued to act the part of a parent state; we felt ourselves happy in our connection with her, nor wished it to be dissolved; but our sentiments are altered, it is now the ardent wish of our soul that America may become a free and independent state.

After a summary of grievances committed by Great Britain, the Malden resolution ended with these paragraphs. Note an echo of Thomas Paine's belief in republican government and his rejection of monarchy.

Source: William Dudley, ed., *op. cit.*, p. 131.

For these reasons, as well as many others which might be produced, we are confirmed in the opinion, that the present age would be deficient in their duty to God, their posterity and themselves, if they do not establish an American republic. This is the only form of government which we wish to see established; for we can never be willingly subject to any other King than he who, being possessed of infinite wisdom, goodness and rectitude, is alone fit to possess unlimited power.

We have freely spoken our sentiments upon this important subject, but we mean not to dictate; we have unbounded confidence in the wisdom and uprightness of the continental congress: with pleasure we recollect that this affair is under their direction; and we now instruct you, sir, to give them the strongest assurance, that, if they should declare America to be a free and independent republic, your constituents will support and defend the measure, to the last drop of blood, and the last farthing of their treasure.

Richard Henry Lee's Resolutions

On June 7, 1776, Virginia delegate Richard Henry Lee proposed the following three resolutions. For obvious reasons, the first was the most explosive.

Source: Donald Barr Chidsey, *July 4, 1776: The Dramatic Story of the First Four Days of July, 1776*, New York: Crown, 1958, p. 41.

That these United Colonies are, and of a right ought to be, free and independent States, that they are absolved from all allegiance to the British Crown, and that all political connection between them and the State of Great Britain is, and ought to be, totally dissolved.

That it is expedient forthwith to take the most effectual measures for forming foreign Alliances.

That a plan of confederation be prepared and transmitted to the respective Colonies for their consideration and approbation.

Jefferson Drafts a Declaration

Lee's resolutions were debated on June 8 and 10, but Congress was unable to pass them. The preliminary vote was close, however, and on June 11 a committee was chosen to draft a formal Declaration of Independence. Its members were John Adams, Thomas Jefferson, Benjamin Franklin, Roger Sherman, and Robert R. Livingston. The actual drafting of the Declaration was assigned to Jefferson. When his draft was finished, Jefferson submitted it to his fellow committee members for editing. Jefferson wrote this accompanying memo to Franklin, who is believed to have made seven small changes in Jefferson's draft.

Source: Thomas Jefferson, *op. cit.*, p. 404.

TH: J. TO DOCTR. FRANKLYN   Friday morn.

[21 June 1776?]

The inclosed paper has been read and with some small alterations approved of by the committee. Will Doctr. Franklyn be so good as to peruse it and suggest such alterations as his more enlarged view of the subject will dictate? The paper having been returned to me to change a particular sentiment or two, I propose laying it again before the committee tomorrow morning, if Doctr. Franklyn can think of it before that time.

John Dickinson's Plea

Debate over Lee's resolutions resumed on July 1, 1776. Pennsylvania delegate John Dickinson, a revered and distinguished leader in the Congress, argued against independence. In the following excerpt from his speech, Dickinson insisted that the colonies weren't ready to rule themselves in harmony.

Source: William Dudley, ed., *op. cit.*, pp. 133-5. (Citation by Dudley: Hezekiah Niles, ed., Principles and Acts of the Revolution in America, Baltimore, 1822.)

Now, it is an established fact that America can be well and happily governed by the English laws, under the same king and the same Parliament. Two hundred years of happiness furnish the proof of it; and we find it also in the present prosperity, which is the result of these venerable laws and of this ancient union. It is not as independent, but as subjects; not as republic, but as monarchy, that we have arrived at this degree of power and of greatness. What then is the object of these chimeras, hatched in the days of discord and war? Shall the transports of fury have more power over us than the experience of ages? Shall we destroy, in a moment of anger, the work cemented and tested by time?

I know the name of liberty is dear to each one of us; but have we not enjoyed liberty even under the English monarchy? Shall we this day renounce that to go and seek it in I know not what form of republic, which will soon change into a licentious anarchy and popular tyranny? In the human body the head only sustains and governs all the members, directing them, with admirable harmony, to the same object, which is self-preservation and happiness; so the head of the body politic, that is the king, in concert with the Parliament, can alone maintain the union of the members of this Empire, lately so flourishing, and prevent civil war by obviating all the evils produced by variety of opinions and diversity of interests....

Even when the powerful hand of England supported us, for the paltry motives of territorial limits and distant jurisdictions, have we not abandoned ourselves to discords, and sometimes even to violence? And what must we not expect, now that minds are heated, ambitions roused, and arms in the hands of all?

Later in his speech, Dickinson made even more explicit his objections to the democratic, anti-monarchical ideas promoted by the likes of Thomas Paine.

Source: William Dudley, ed., *op. cit.*, pp. 137-8.

There are many persons who, to gain their ends, extol the advantages of a republic over monarchy. I will not here undertake to examine which of these two forms of government merits the preference. I know, however, that the English nation, after having tried them both, has never found repose except in monarchy. I know, also, that in popular republics themselves, so necessary is monarchy to cement human society, it has been requisite to institute monarchical powers, more or less extensive, under the names of *archons*, of *consuls*, of *doges*, of *gonfaloniers*, and finally of *kings*. Nor should I here omit an observation, the truth of which appears to me incontestable-the English constitution seems to be the fruit of the experience of all anterior time, in which monarchy is so tempered that the monarch finds himself checked in his efforts to seize absolute power; and the authority of the people is so regulated that anarchy is not to be feared. But for us it is to be apprehended that, when the counterpoise of monarchy shall no longer exist, the democratic power may carry all before it and involve the whole state in confusion and ruin. Then an ambitious citizen may arise, seize the reins of power, and annihilate liberty forever; for such is the ordinary career of ill-balanced democracies, they fall into anarchy, and thence under despotism.

John and Abigail Adams:
Hope and Apprehension

Abigail Adams   *John Adams*

Despite Dickinson's plea, Congress voted in favor of independence on July 2. On July 3, 1776, John Adams wrote the following to his wife, Abigail, in Boston.

Source: Abigail Adams and John Adams, *The Book of Abigail and John: Selected Letters of the Adams Family, 1762-1784,* eds. L. H. Butterfield, Marc Friedlaender, and Mary-Jo Kline; Cambridge, MA: Harvard Press, 1975, pp. 139-40.

Yesterday the greatest Question was decided, which ever was debated in America, and a greater perhaps, never was or will be decided among Men. A Resolution was passed with out one dissenting Colony "that these united Colonies, are, and of right ought to be free and independent States, and as such, they have, and of Right ought to have full Power to make War, conclude Peace, establish Commerce, and to do all the other Acts and Things, which other States may rightfully do." You will see in a few days a Declaration setting forth the Causes, which have impell'd Us to this mighty Revolution, and the Reasons which will justify it, in the Sight of God and Man. A Plan of Confederation will be taken up in a few days.

When I look back to the Year 1761...I am surprized at the Suddenness, as well as Greatness of this Revolution. Britain has been fill'd with Folly, and America with Wisdom, at least this is my Judgment. — Time must determine. It is the Will of Heaven, that the two Countries should be sundered forever. It may be the Will of Heaven that America shall suffer Calamities still more wasting and Distresses yet more dreadfull. If this is to be the Case, it will have this good Effect, at least: it will inspire Us with many Virtues, which We have not, and correct many Errors, Follies, and Vices, which threaten to disturb, dishonour, and destroy Us. — The Furnace of Affliction produces Refinement, in States as well as Individuals. And the new Governments we are assuming, in every Part, will require a Purification from our Vices, and an Augmentation of our Virtues or they will be no Blessings. The People will have unbounded Power. And the People are extreamly addicted to Corruption and Venality, as well as the Great. — I am not without Apprehensions from this Quarter. But I must submit all my Hopes and Fears, to an overruling Providence, in which, unfashionable as the Faith may be, I firmly believe.

Later the same day, Adams made the following famous prophecy in another letter to his wife. Note his assumption that July 2, not July 4, would be celebrated as Independence Day.

Source: Abigail Adams and John Adams, *op. cit.*, p. 142.

The Second Day of July 1776, will be the most memorable Epocha, in the History of America. — I am apt to believe it will be celebrated, by succeeding Generations, as the great anniversary Festival. It ought to be commemorated, as the Day of Deliverance by solemn Acts of Devotion to God Almighty. It ought to be solemnized with Pomp and Parade, with Shews, Games, Sports, Guns, Bells, Bonfires and Illuminations from one End of this Continent to the other from this Time forward forever more.

You will think me transported with Enthusiasm but I am not. — I am well aware of the Toil and Blood and Treasure, that it will cost Us to maintain this Declaration, and support and defend these States. — Yet through all the Gloom I can see the Rays of ravishing Light and Glory. I can see that the End is more than worth all the Means. And that Posterity will tryumph in that Days Transaction, even altho We should rue it, which I trust in God We shall not.

On July 13, Abigail Adams made the following proud reply.

Source: Abigail Adams and John Adams, *op. cit.*, p. 145.

By yesterdays post I received two Letters dated 3 and 4 of July and tho your Letters never fail to give me pleasure, be the subject what it will, yet it was greatly heightned by the prospect of the future happiness and glory of our Country; nor am I a little Gratified when I reflect that a person so nearly connected with me has had the Honour of being a principal actor, in laying a foundation for its future Greatness. May the foundation of our new constitution, be justice, Truth and Righteousness. Like the wise Mans house may it be founded upon those Rocks and then neither storms or temptests will overthrow it.

Benjamin Franklin and John Thompson's Hats

After voting for indepence on July 2, Congress began to edit and revise the document prepared by Thomas Jefferson and the drafting committee. Historians have generally agreed that these changes (dealt with in the next chapter) improved the Declaration. But Jefferson was horrified. While this editing unfolded, he received some good-humored solace from Benjamin Franklin, which he described in an 1818 letter to Robert Walsh.

Source: Thomas Jefferson, *The Life and Selected Writings of Thomas Jefferson*, eds. Adrienne Koch and William Peden, New York: Random House, 1984, pp. 168.

I was sitting by Dr. Franklin, who perceived that I was not insensible to these mutilations. "I have made it a rule," said he, "whenever in my power, to avoid becoming the draughtsman of papers to be reviewed by a public body. I took my lesson from an incident which I will relate to you. When I was a journeyman printer, one of my companions, an apprentice hatter, having served out his time, was about to open shop for himself. His first concern was to have a handsome signboard, with a proper inscription. He composed it in these words, 'John Thompson, *Hatter, makes* and *sells hats* for ready money,' with a figure of a hat subjoined; but he thought he would submit it to his friends for their amendments. The first he showed it to thought the word '*Hatter*' tautologous, because followed by the words 'makes hats,' which show he was a hatter. It was struck out. The next observed that the word '*makes*' might as well be omitted, because his customers would not care who made the hats. If good and to their mind, they would buy, by whomsoever made. He struck it out. A third said he thought the words '*for ready money*' were useless, as it was not the custom of the place to sell on credit. Every one who purchased expected to pay. They were parted with, and the inscription now stood, 'John Thompson sells hats.' '*Sells hats!*' says his next friend. Why nobody will expect you to give them away, what then is the use of that word? It was stricken out, and '*hats*' followed it, the rather as there was one painted on the board. So the inscription was reduced ultimately to 'John Thompson' with the figure of a hat subjoined."

The Declaration of Independence

On July 4, Congress was satisfied with the Declaration and voted to adopt it. The finished document opened with these memorable words.

Source: Thomas Jefferson, *op. cit.*, pp. 429-30.

When in the Course of human events, it becomes necessary for one people to dissolve the political bands which have connected them with another, and to assume among the powers of the earth, the separate and equal station to which the Laws of Nature and of Nature's God entitle them, a decent respect to the opinions of mankind requires that they should declare the causes which impel them to the separation.

We hold these truths to be self-evident, that all men are created equal, that they are endowed by their Creator with certain unalienable Rights, that among these are Life, Liberty and the pursuit of Happiness. That to secure these rights, Governments are instituted among Men, deriving their just powers from the consent of the governed, That whenever any Form of Government becomes destructive of these ends, it is the Right of the People to alter or to abolish it, and to institute new Government, laying its foundation on such principles and organizing its powers in such form, as to them shall seem most likely to effect their Safety and Happiness. Prudence, indeed, will dictate that Governments long established should not be changed for light and transient causes; and accordingly all experience hath shewn, that mankind are more disposed to suffer, while evils are sufferable, than to right themselves by abolishing the forms to which they are accustomed. But when a long train of abuses and usurpations, pursuing invariably the same Object evinces a design to reduce them under absolute Despotism, it is their right, it is their duty, to throw off such Government, and to provide new Guards for their future security. Such has been the patient sufferance of these Colonies; and such is now the necessity which constrains them to alter their former Systems of Government. The history of the present King of Great Britain is a history of repeated injuries and usurpations, all having in direct object the establishment of an absolute Tyranny over these States. To prove this, let Facts be submitted to a candid world.

The Declaration continued with the following grievances against Great Britain — a passage which is read less often today than the paragraphs above, but which, in 1776, were by far the most vital parts of the document. (The concluding paragraphs of the Declaration will be dealt with in the next chapter.)

Source: Thomas Jefferson, *op. cit.*, pp. 430-1.

He has refused his Assent to Laws, the most wholesome and necessary for the public good.

He has forbidden his Governors to pass Laws of immediate and pressing importance, unless suspended in their operation till his Assent should be obtained; and when so suspended, he has utterly neglected to attend to them.

He has refused to pass other Laws for the accommodation of large districts of people, unless those people would relinquish the right of Representation in the Legislature, a right inestimable to them and formidable to tyrants only.

He has called together legislative bodies at places unusual, uncomfortable, and distant from the depository of their Public Records, for the sole purpose of fatiguing them into compliance with his measures.

He has dissolved Representative Houses repeatedly, for opposing with manly firmness his invasions on the rights of the people.

He has refused for a long time, after such dissolutions, to cause others to be elected; whereby the Legislative Powers, incapable of Annihilation, have returned to the People at large for their exercise; the State remaining in the mean time exposed to all the dangers of invasion from without, and convulsions from within.

He has endeavoured to prevent the population of these States; for that purpose obstructing the Laws of Naturalization of Foreigners; refusing to pass others to encourage their migration hither, and raising the conditions of new Appropriations of Lands.

He has obstructed the Administration of Justice, by refusing his Assent to Laws for establishing Judiciary Powers.

He has made Judges dependent on his Will alone, for the tenure of their offices, and the amount and payment of their salaries.

He has erected a multitude of New Offices, and sent hither swarms of Officers to harass our People, and eat out their substance.

He has kept among us, in times of peace, Standing Armies without the Consent of our legislatures.

He has affected to render the Military independent of and superior to the Civil Power.

He has combined with others to subject us to a jurisdiction foreign to our constitution, and unacknowledged by our laws; giving his Assent to their acts of pretended legislation;

For quartering large bodies of armed troops among us:

For protecting them, by a mock Trial, from Punishment for any Murders which they should commit on the Inhabitants of these States:

For cutting off our Trade with all parts of the world:

For imposing Taxes on us without our Consent:

For depriving us in many cases, of the benefits of Trial by Jury:

For transporting us beyond Seas to be tried for pretended offences:

For abolishing the free System of English Laws in a neighbouring Province, establishing therein an Arbitrary government, and enlarging its Boundaries so as to render it at once an example and fit instrument for introducing the same absolute rule into these Colonies:

For taking away our Charters, abolishing our most valuable Laws, and altering fundamentally the Forms of our Governments:

For suspending our own Legislatures, and declaring themselves invested with Power to legislate for us in all cases whatsoever.

He has abdicated Government here, by declaring us out of his Protection and waging War against us.

He has plundered our seas, ravaged our Coasts, burnt our towns, and destroyed the Lives of our people.

He is at this time transporting large armies of foreign mercenaries to compleat the works of death, desolation and tyranny, already begun with circumstances of Cruelty & perfidy scarcely paralleled in the most barbarous ages, and totally unworthy the Head of a civilized nation.

He has constrained our fellow Citizens taken Captive on the high Seas to bear Arms against their Country, to become the executioners of their friends and Brethren, or to fall themselves by their Hands.

He has excited domestic insurrections amongst us, and had endeavoured to bring on the inhabitants of the our frontiers, the merciless Indian Savages, whose known rule of warfare, is an undistinguished destruction of all ages, sexes and conditions.

The End of Royal Authority

Several days later, Abigail Adams heard the document read in Boston. She described the event in a July 21 letter to her husband.

Source: Abigail Adams and John Adams, *op. cit.*, p. 148.

Last Thursday after hearing a very Good Sermon I went with the Multitude into Kings Street to hear the proclamation for independance read and proclamed. Some Field peices with the Train were brought there, the troops appeard under Arms and all the inhabitants assembled there (the small pox prevented many thousand from the Country). When Col. Crafts read from the Belcona of the State House the Proclamation, great attention was given to every word. As soon as he ended, the cry from the Belcona, was God Save our American States and then 3 cheers which rended the air, the Bells rang, the privateers fired, the forts and Batteries, the cannon were discharged, the platoons followed and every face appeard joyfull. Mr. Bowdoin then gave a Sentiment, Stability and perpetuity to American independance. After dinner the kings arms were taken down from the State House and every vestage of him from every place in which it appeard and burnt in King Street. Thus ends royall Authority in this State, and all the people shall say Amen.

"Pursuit of Happiness?"

Understandably, many British reactions to the Declaration of Independence were hardly favorable. For example, an anonymous writer raised this complaint regarding one of the Declaration's most famous phrases.

Source: Garry Wills, *Inventing America: Jefferson's Declaration of Independence*, New York: Doubleday, 1978, p. 246. (Citation by Wills: Scots Magazine, August 1776.)

Did ever any mortal alive hear of taking a pursuit of happiness from a man? What they possibly can mean by these words,

I own is beyond my comprehension. A man may take from me a horse or a cow, or I may alienate either of them from myself, as I may likewise anything that I have; but how that can be taken from me, or alienated, which I have not, must be left for the solution of some unborn Oedipus.[2]

Edmund Burke

Some of the finest British thinkers felt differently. Statesman and political philosopher Edmund Burke, for example, made a speech to parliament on November 6, 1776 to protest continued British hostilities and an edict to pray against the colonial cause. He directed this address to England's Solicitor General Alexander Wedderburn. The following excerpts are from his speech.

Source: Edmund Burke, *Edmund Burke On the American Revolution*, ed. Elliott R. Barkan, New York: Harper Torchbooks, 1966, pp. 139-40. (Unbracketed ellipses are in Barkan's text; bracketed ellipses indicate deletions by the editor of this volume.)

Witness the behaviour of one miserable woman who, with her single arm, did that which an army of a hundred thousand men could not do — arrested your progress in the moment of your success. This miserable being was found in a cellar, with her visage besmeared and smutted over, with every mark of rage, despair, resolution, and the most *exalted heroism, buried* in combustibles, in order to fire New York and perish in its *ashes.* She was brought forth and, knowing that she would be condemned to die, upon being asked her purpose, said, "to fire the city!" and was determined to omit no opportunity of doing what her country called for. Her train was laid and fired; and it is worthy of your attention how Providence was pleased to make use of those humble means to serve the American cause, when open force was used in vain. In order to bring things to this unhappy situation, did not you pave the way, by a succession of acts of tyranny? For this you shut up their ports, cut off their fishery, annihilated their charter, and governed them by

---

[2] A character in Greek mythology known for solving riddles.

an army. Sir, the recollection of these things, being the evident causes of what we have seen, is more than what *ought* to be *endured*. This it is that has *burnt* the noble city of New York, that has planted the bayonet in the bosoms of my principals — in the bosom of the city where alone your wretched government once boasted the only friends she could number in America. If this was not the only succession of events you determined, and therefore looked for, why was America left without any power in it, to give security to the persons and property of those who were and wished to be loyal — this was essential to government. You did not, and might therefore be well said to have abdicated government.

…Gods! Sir, shall we be told that you cannot analyze grievances? — that you can have no communication with rebels because they have declared for independency? […] You simply tell them to lay down their arms and then you will do just as you please. Could the most cruel conqueror say less? Had you conquered the devil himself in hell, could you be less liberal? No! Sir, you would offer no terms. You meant to drive them to the declaration of independency; and even after it was issued, ought by your offers to have reversed the effect. […]

In this situation, Sir, shocking to say, are we called upon by another proclamation to go to the altar of the Almighty, with war and vengeance in our hearts, instead of the peace of our blessed Saviour. He said, "My peace I give you." But we are, on this fast, to have war only in our hearts and mouths, war against our brethren. Till our churches are purified from this abominable service, I shall consider them, not as the temples of the Almighty, but the synagogues of Satan. An act not more *infamous*, respecting its political purposes, than *blasphemous* and *profane* as a pretended act of national devotion, when the people are called upon, in the most solemn and awful manner, to repair to church, to partake of a sacrament, and, at the foot of the altar, to commit sacrilege, to perjure themselves publicly by charging their American brethren with the horrid crime of rebellion, with propagating "specious falsehoods," when either the charge must be *notoriously false*, or those who make it, not knowing it to be true, call Almighty God to witness — not a *specious* but — as most *audacious* and *blasphemous* falsehood.

Josiah Tucker

The British political thinker Josiah Tucker also favored American independence— primarily because he despised the colonists and their democratic ideals. He wrote the following in a letter to the British prime minister in 1783.

Source: Max Beloff, ed., *The Debate on the American Revolution: 1761-1783*, Dobbs Ferry, New York: Sheridan House, 1989, pp. 297-9.

As to *America*, and the Resistance which this honourable *Fraternity* [3] have so strenuously excited throughout that Country, I am as glad of the *general Event*, though *not of the particular Circumstances attending it*, as the most flaming Republicans. — I say, I am glad that *America* had declared herself independent of us, though for Reasons very opposite to theirs. *America*, I have proved beyond the Possibility of a Confutation, ever was a Millstone hanging about the Neck of this Country, to weigh it down: And as we ourselves had not the Wisdom to cut the Rope, and to let the Burthen fall off, the Americans have kindly done it for us. The only Thing to be lamented, which never can be lamented enough, was, that as soon as this ungrateful People had refused to pass a public Vote for contributing *any Thing*, or in *any Mode*, towards the general Expence of the Empire, but on the contrary, had entered into Combinations to forbid the Importation of our Manufactures, we had not taken them at their Word, and totally cast them off. Had we done this, it would have been happy for us; nay, it would have been happy for *them* too: Because this would have saved both them and us that Blood and Treasure, which have been so profusely lavished for many Years, without answering any one End whatever....

---

[3] i.e., British supporters of the American cause.

Thomas Jefferson and His Ideas

In crucial ways, the Declaration of Independence was a collaborative document. Thomas Jefferson worked on it under strict instructions from the Continental Congress and with close assistance from John Adams and Benjamin Franklin. And of course, Congress revised it considerably. At the same time, the initial drafting of the Declaration essentially fell to him, and it reflects his own thoughts about government and human nature. For this reason, it is worthwhile to take a look at Jefferson and his ideas.

Jefferson's "Summary View"

Jefferson's "A Summary View of the Rights of British America," written in 1774 as instructions for the Virginia delegation to Congress, concluded with this passionate appeal to the English king — not as a ruler but as an equal power. Although this document was published in both America and England, it was never officially used in Congress as Jefferson had hoped.

Source: Thomas Jefferson, *Writings*, ed. Merrill D. Peterson, New York: Library of America, 1984, pp. 120-2.

That these are our grievances which we have thus laid before his majesty, with that freedom of language and sentiment which becomes a free people claiming their rights, as derived from the laws of nature, and not as the gift of their chief magistrate: Let those flatter who fear; it is not an American art. To give praise which is not due might be well from the venal, but would ill beseem those who are asserting the rights of human nature. They know, and will therefore say, that kings are the servants, not the proprietors of the people. Open your breast, sire, to liberal and expanded thought. Let not the name of George the third be a blot in the page of history. You are surrounded by

British counsellors, but remember that they are parties. You have no ministers for American affairs, because you have none taken from among us, nor amenable to the laws on which they are to give you advice. It behoves you, therefore, to think and to act for yourself and your people. The great principles of right and wrong are legible to every reader; to pursue them requires not the aid of many counsellors. The whole art of government consists in the art of being honest. Only aim to do your duty, and mankind will give you credit where you fail. No longer persevere in sacrificing the rights of one part of the empire to the inordinate desires of another; but deal out to all equal and impartial right. Let no act be passed by any one legislature which may infringe on the rights and liberties of another. This is the important post in which fortune has placed you, holding the balance of a great, if a well poised empire. This, sire, is the advice of your great American council, on the observance of which may perhaps depend your felicity and future fame, and the preservation of that harmony which alone can continue both to Great Britain and America the reciprocal advantages of their connection. It is neither our wish, nor our interest, to separate from her. We are willing, on our part, to sacrifice every thing which reason can ask to the restoration of that tranquillity for which all must wish. On their part, let them be ready to establish union and a generous plan. Let them name their terms, but let them be just....The God who gave us life gave us liberty at the same time; the hand of force may destroy, but cannot disjoin them. This, sire, is our last, our determined resolution; and that you will be pleased to interpose with that efficacy which your earnest endeavours may ensure to procure redress of these our great grievances, to quiet the minds of your subjects in British America, against any apprehensions of future encroachment, to establish fraternal love and harmony through the whole empire, and that these may continue to the latest ages of time, is the fervent prayer of all British America!

The Tree of Liberty

When Jefferson wrote in the Declaration that people have the power to "alter or to abolish" undesired governments, he believed it more passionately than most of his contemporaries did. To him, even civil violence seemed a small price to pay for shaking up the status quo.

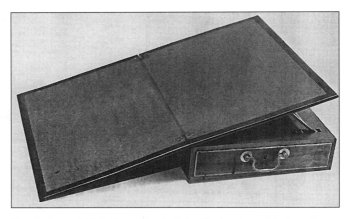

The desk at which Jefferson drafted the Declaration of Independence, designed by himself for portability and convenience. (Smithsonian)

In 1786, a Revolutionary War veteran named Daniel Shays led a small but violent rebellion against taxes in Massachusetts. The rebellion was quickly put down, but many influential people were deeply frightened by it. By contrast, Jefferson wrote the following in a letter to William S. Smith in 1787.

Source: Thomas Jefferson, *op. cit.*, p. 911.

And can history produce an instance of rebellion so honourably conducted? I say nothing of it's motives. They were founded in ignorance, not wickedness. God forbid we should ever be 20 years without such a rebellion. The people cannot be all, & always, well informed. The part which is wrong will be discontented in proportion to the importance of the facts they misconceive. If they remain quiet under such misconceptions it is a lethargy, a forerunner of death to the public liberty. We have had 13. states independent 11. years. There has been one rebellion. That comes to one rebellion in a century & a half for each state. What country before ever existed a century & half without a rebellion? & what country can preserve it's liberties if their rulers are not warned from time to time that their people preserve the spirit of resistance? Let them take arms. The remedy is to set them right as to facts, pardon & pacify them. What signify a few lives lost in a century or two? The tree of liberty must be refreshed from time to time with the blood of patriots & tyrants. It is it's natural manure.

The Pursuit of Happiness

Jefferson greatly revered the English philosopher John Locke. Jefferson's phrase "life, liberty & the pursuit of happiness" is often traced back to Locke's Second Treatise of Government. *But in that work, Locke's terms were life, liberty, and property (or estate). Why did Jefferson change "property" to "the pursuit of happiness?" In using this phrase, Jefferson seems to have echoed a different work by Locke:* An Essay Concerning Human Understanding.

Source: John Locke, *An Essay Concerning Human Understanding,* ed. Peter H. Nidditch, Oxford: Clarendon, 1975, pp. 265-7.

The constant desire of Happiness, and the constraint it puts upon us to act for it, no Body, I think, accounts an abridgment of *Liberty,* or at least an abridgment of *Liberty* to be complain'd of. God Almighty himself is under the necessity of being happy; and the more any intelligent Being is so, the nearer is its approach to infinite perfection and happiness. That in this state of Ignorance we short-sighted Creatures might not mistake true felicity, we are endowed with a power to suspend any particular desire, and keep it from determining the *will,* and engaging us in action. This is *standing still,* where we are not sufficiently assured of the way: Examination is *consulting a guide*. The determination of the *will* upon enquiry is *following the direction of that Guide*: And he that has a power to act, or not to act according as such determination directs, is a *free Agent*: such determination abridges not the Power wherein Liberty consists. He that has his Chains knocked off, and the Prison-door set open to him, is perfectly at *liberty*, because he may either go or stay, as he best likes; though his preference be determined to stay, by the darkness of the Night, or illness of the Weather, or want of other Lodging. He ceases not to be free; though the desire of some convenience to be had there, absolutely determines his preference, and makes him stay in his Prison.

As therefore the highest perfection of intellectual nature, lies in a careful and constant pursuit of true and solid happiness; so the care of our selves, that we mistake not imaginary for real happiness, is the necessary foundation of our *liberty*. The stronger ties, we have, to an unalterable pursuit of happiness in general, which is our greatest good, and which as such our desires always follow, the more are we free from any necessary determination of our *will* to any particular action, and from a necessary compliance with our desire, set upon any particular, and then appearing preferable good, till we have duly examin'd, whether it has a tendency to, or be inconsistent with our real happiness; and therefore till we are as much inform'd upon this enquiry, as the weight of the matter, and the nature of the case demands, we are by the necessity of prefering and pursuing true happiness as our greatest good, obliged to suspend the satisfaction of our desire in particular cases.

This is the hinge on which turns the *liberty* of intellectual Beings in their constant endeavours after, and a steady prosecution of true felicity, that they can *suspend* this prosecution in particular cases, till they have looked before them, and informed themselves, whether that particular thing, which is then proposed, or desired, like in the way to their main end, and make a real part of that which is their greatest good.

The Equality of Man

Thomas Jefferson

What did Jefferson mean when he wrote "all men are created equal?" According to historian Garry Wills (from Inventing America: Jefferson's Declaration of Independence), *Jefferson's ideas about equality were based on the "moral-sense" theory of his day. He explains in this passage from a 1787 letter to his nephew Peter Carr.*

Source: Thomas Jefferson, *op. cit.*, pp. 901-2.

He who made us would have been a pitiful bungler if he had made the rules of our moral conduct a matter of science. For one man of science, there are thousands who are not. What would have become of them? Man was destined for society. His morality therefore was to be formed to this object. He was endowed with a sense of right & wrong merely relative to this. This sense is as much a part of his nature as the sense of hearing, seeing, feeling; it is the true foundation of morality....The moral sense, or conscience, is as much a part of man as his leg or arm. It is given to all human beings in a stronger or weaker degree, as force of members is given them in a greater or less degree. It may be strengthened by exercise, as may any particular limb of the body. This sense is submitted indeed in some degree to the guidance of reason; but it is a small stock which is required for this: even a less one than what we call common sense. State a moral case to a ploughman & a professor. The former will decide it as well, & often better than the latter, because he has not been led astray by artificial rules.

Natural Aristocracy

Although Jefferson claimed a certain moral equality for all men, he admitted that they differed in innate abilities and talents. But this did not justify granting them unequal social rights, as Jefferson argued in an 1813 letter to his more conservative friend John Adams.

Source: Thomas Jefferson, *op. cit.*, 1305-6.

For I agree with you that there is a natural aristocracy among men. The grounds of this are virtue and talents. Formerly bodily powers gave place among the aristoi. But since the invention of gunpowder has armed the weak as well as the strong with missile death, bodily strength, like beauty, good humor, politeness and other accomplishments, has become but an auxiliary ground of distinction. There is also an artificial aristocracy founded on wealth and birth, without either virtue or talents; for with these it would belong to the first class. The natural aristocracy I consider as the most precious gift of nature for the instruction, the trusts, and government of society. And indeed it would have been inconsistent in creation to have formed man for the social state, and not to have provided virtue and wisdom enough to manage the concerns of the society. May we not even say that the form of government is the best which provides the most effectually for a pure selection of these natural aristoi into the offices of government? The artificial aristocracy is a mischievous ingredient in government, and provision should be made to prevent it's ascendancy....

I think the best remedy is exactly that provided by all our constitutions, to leave to the citizens the free election and separation of the aristoi from the pseudo-aristoi, of the wheat from the chaff. In general they will elect the real good and wise. In some instances, wealth may corrupt, and birth blind them; but not in sufficient degree to endanger the society.

The Parts Left Out of Jefferson's Declaration

The Declaration actually adopted by Congress had been altered from the version prepared by Jefferson, Adams, and Franklin. The famous preamble was changed very slightly, but the closing paragraphs were considerably cut and revised. For the rest of his life, Jefferson felt that these changes had weakened the document. He issued a version of the Declaration which merged both his and Congress' versions so that posterity could see the difference.

The following passage comes immediately after the list of grievances (see previous chapter). Bracketed, underlined passages were written by Jefferson but cut by Congress. Words and phrases in the margin were added by Congress.

Source: Garry Wills, *op. cit.*, pp. 377-8. (Citation by Wills: Julian P. Boyd et al., eds., *The Papers of Thomas Jefferson*, Princeton, 1950-74, Vol. 1, pp. 315-19.)

In every stage of these oppressions we have petitioned for redress in the most humble terms: our repeated petitions have been answered only by repeated injuries. A prince whose character is thus marked by every act which may define a tyrant is unfit to be the ruler of a ^ people [who mean   ^ free
to be free. Future ages will scarcely believe that the hardiness of one man adventured, within the short compass of twelve years only, to lay a foundation so broad & so undisguised for tyranny over a people fostered & fixed in principles of freedom.]

Nor have we been wanting in attentions to our British brethren. We have warned them from time to time of attempts by their legislature to extend ^   ^ an unwarrantable
[a] jurisdiction over ^ [these our states.] We have   ^ us
reminded them of the circumstances of our emigration & settlement here, [no one of which could warrant so strange a pretension: that these were effected at the expence of our own blood & treasure, unassisted by the wealth or the strength of Great Britain: that in constituting indeed our several

forms of government, we had adopted one common king, thereby laying a foundation for perpetual league & amity with them: but that submission to their parliament was no part of our constitution, nor ever in idea, if history may be credited: and,] we ^ appealed to their native justice and magnanimity ^ [as well as to] the ties of our common kindred to disavow these usurpations which ^ [were likely to] interrupt our connection and correspondence. They too have been deaf to the voice of justice & of consanguinity, [and when occasions have been given them, by the regular course of their laws, of removing from their councils the disturbers of our harmony, they have, by their free election, re-established them in power. At this very time too they are permitting their chief magistrate to send over not only souldiers of our common blood, but Scotch & foreign mercenaries to invade & destroy us. These facts have given the last stab to agonizing affection, and manly spirit bids us to renounce for ever these unfeeling brethren. We must endeavor to forget our former love for them, and to hold them as we hold the rest of mankind enemies in war, in peace friends. We might have been a free and great people together; but a communication of grandeur & of freedom it seems is below their dignity. Be it so, since they will have it. The road to happiness & to glory is open to us too. We will tread it apart from them, and] ^ acquiesce in the necessity which denounces our [eternal] separation ^ !

^ have

^ and we have conjured them by

^ would inevitably

^ we must therefore

^ and hold them as we hold the rest of mankind, enemies in war, in peace friends.

The closing of the Declaration was so altered that Jefferson found it necessary to put it into two separate columns. On the left is his version; on the right is Congress's. Note that Jefferson was less inclined to invoke the assistance of divine providence than his political colleagues. Also note that Jefferson's actual renunciation of British authority was replaced by the language of Richard Henry Lee's resolution (see previous chapter).

Source: Garry Wills, *op. cit.*, p. 379.

We therefore the representatives of the United states of America in General Congress assembled do in the name, & by the authority of the good people of these [states reject & renounce all allegiance & subjection to the kings of Great Britain & all others who may hereafter claim by, through or under them: we utterly dissolve all political connection which may heretofore have subsisted between us & the people or parliament of Great Britain: & finally we do assert & declare these colonies to be free & independant states,] & that as free & independant states, they have full power to levy war, conclude peace, contract alliances, establish commerce, & to do all other acts & things which independant states may of right do. And for the support of this declaration we mutually pledge to each other our lives, our fortunes & our sacred honour.

We therefore the representatives of the United states of America in General Congress assembled, appealing to the supreme judge of the world for the rectitude of our intentions, do in the name, & by the authority of the good people of these colonies, solemnly publish and declare that these United colonies are & of right ought to be free & independant states; that they are absolved from all allegiance to the British crown, and that all political connection between them & the state of Great Britain is, & ought to be, totally dissolved; & that as free & independant states they have full power to levy war, conclude peace, contract alliances, establish commerce & to do all other acts & things which independant states may of right do. And for the support of this declaration, with a firm reliance on the protection of divine providence we mutually pledge to each other our lives, our fortunes & our sacred honour.

The Clause on Slavery

Congress also cut an earlier paragraph from Jefferson's list of grievances on the subject of slavery. Legend holds that Jefferson wrote it with the intention of ridding America of slavery once and for all, only to be thwarted by his fellow Southerners. But the Declaration was intended as a revolutionary tract, not the law of the land; Jefferson could not have used it to eliminate slavery.

The entire excised paragraph follows. Note that Jefferson did not argue against slavery so much as he did against the slave trade — especially England's role in its perpetuation. Disturbingly, he ended this paragraph by condemning England for freeing slaves who fought against the colonists.

Source: Garry Wills, *op. cit.*, p. 377.

He has waged cruel war against human nature itself, violating it's most sacred rights of life and liberty in the persons of a distant people who never offended him, captivating & carrying them into slavery in another hemisphere or to incur miserable death in their transportation thither. This piratical warfare, the opprobrium of *infidel* powers, is the warfare of the *Christian* king of Great Britain. Determined to keep open a market where *Men* should be bought & sold, he has prostituted his negative for suppressing every legislative attempt to prohibit or to restrain this execrable commerce. And that this assemblage of horrors might want no fact of distinguished die, he is now exciting those very people to rise in arms among us, and to purchase that liberty of which he has deprived them, by murdering the people on whom he also obtruded them: thus paying off former crimes committed against the *Liberties* of one people, with crimes which he urges them to commit against the *lives* of another.

Jefferson on Slavery

To generations of readers, the subject of slavery has cast a shadow over the Declaration of Independence and its claim of human equality. Jefferson himself was a slave owner who unsuccessfully tried to pass legislation in Virginia to bring a gradual end to slavery. His plan was (on a certain date and at public expense) to begin educating and training all newborn slaves for freedom. As they reached adulthood, African-Americans would be sent away to a colony of their own. The following passage from Jefferson's book, Notes on the State of Virginia, *published in 1787, came after his description of this scheme.*

Source: Thomas Jefferson, *Writings*, pp. 264-6.

It will probably be asked, Why not retain and incorporate the blacks into the state, and thus save the expence of supplying, by importation of white settlers, the vacancies they will leave? Deep rooted prejudices entertained by the whites; ten thousand recollections, by the blacks, of the injuries they have sustained; new provocations; the real distinctions which nature has made; and many other circumstances, will divide us into parties, and produce convulsions which will probably never end but in the extermination of the one or the other race. — To these objections, which are political, may be added others, which are physical and moral. The first difference which strikes us is that of colour. Whether the black of the negro resides in the reticular membrane between the skin and scarf-skin, or in the scarf-skin itself; whether it proceeds from the colour of the blood, the colour of the bile, or from that of some other secretion, the difference is fixed in nature, and is as real as if its seat and cause were better known to us. And is this difference of no importance? Is it not the foundation of greater or less share of beauty in the two races? Are not the fine mixtures of red and white, the expressions of every passion by greater or less suffusions of colour in the one, preferable to that eternal monotony, which reigns in the countenances, that immovable veil of black which covers all the emotions of the other race? Add to these, flowing hair, a more elegant symmetry of form, their own judgment in favour of the whites, declared by their preference of them, as uniformly as is the preference of the Oranootan for the black women over those of his own species.[4] The circumstance of superior beauty, is thought worthy attention in the propagation of our horses, dogs, and other domestic animals; why not in that of man? Besides those of colour, figure, and hair, there are other physical distinctions proving a difference of race. They have less hair on the face and body. They secrete less by the kidnies, and more by the glands of the skin, which gives them a very strong and disagreeable odour. This greater degree of transpiration renders them more tolerant of heat, and less so of cold, than the whites.…They seem to require less sleep. A black, after hard labour through the day, will be induced by the slightest amusements to sit up till midnight, or later, though knowing he must be out with the first dawn of the morning. They are at least as brave, and more adventuresome. But this may perhaps proceed from a want of forethought, which prevents their seeing a danger till it be present. When present, they do not go through it with more coolness or steadiness than the whites. They are more ardent after their female: but love seems with them to be more an eager desire, than a tender delicate mixture of sentiment and sensation. Their griefs are transient. Those numberless afflictions, which render it doubtful whether heaven has given life to us in mercy or in wrath, are less felt, and sooner forgotten with them. In general, their existence appears to participate more of sensation than reflection. To this must be ascribed their disposition to sleep when abstracted from their diversions, and unemployed in labour. An animal

---

[4] Scientists of the eighteenth century believed that humans and orangutans sometimes mated.

whose body is at rest, and who does not reflect, must be disposed to sleep of course. Comparing them by their faculties of memory, reason, and imagination, it appears to me, that in memory they are equal to the whites; in reason much inferior, as I think one could scarcely be found capable of tracing and comprehending the investigations of Euclid; and that in imagination they are dull, tasteless, and anomalous....[N]ever yet could I find that a black had uttered a thought above the level of plain narration; never see even an elementary trait of painting or sculpture. In music they are more generally gifted than the whites with accurate ears for tune and time, and they have been found capable of imagining a small catch.[5] Whether they will be equal to the composition of a more extensive run of melody, or of complicated harmony, is yet to be proved.

In the following passage from the same book, Jefferson qualified his theory of black inferiority. Historian Garry Wills has indicated how crucial this qualification was (Wills, op. cit., 218-28). For according to Jefferson's moral-sense theory, human equality must be based on the heart (the seat of morality), not on the head (the seat of reason).

Source: Thomas Jefferson, *Writings*, pp. 268-9.

Whether further observation will or will not verify the conjecture, that nature has been less bountiful to them in the endowments of the head, I believe that in those of the heart she will be found to have done them justice....[W]e find among them numerous instances of the most rigid integrity, and as many as among their better instructed masters, of benevolence, gratitude, and unshaken fidelity.

---

[5] A three-part song; a round.

Later Thoughts on Race

Today, even the more benign racial ideas stated in Jefferson's Notes on the State of Virginia *seem bizarre, offensive, and unscientific. Indeed, in the same book, Jefferson cautioned that his observations might have little foundation in fact. In 1809, Jefferson wrote a letter to French scholar Henri Gringoire suggesting that he hoped, at long last, to be proven wrong in his theories.*

Source: Thomas Jefferson, *Writings*, p. 1202.

SIR, — I have received the favor of your letter of August 17th, and with it the volume you were so kind as to send me on the "Literature of Negroes." Be assured that no person living wishes more sincerely than I do, to see a complete refutation of the doubts I have myself entertained and expressed on the grade of understanding allotted to them by nature, and to find that in this respect they are on a par with ourselves. My doubts were the result of personal observation on the limited sphere of my own State, where the opportunities for the development of their genius were not favorable, and those of exercising it still less so. I expressed them therefore with great hesitation; but whatever be their degree of talent it is no measure of their rights. Because Sir Isaac Newton was superior to others in understanding, he was not therefore lord of the person or property of others. On this subject they are gaining daily in the opinions of nations, and hopeful advances are making towards their re-establishment on an equal footing with the other colors of the human family....

The Declaration and Posterity

The Declaration of Independence has come down to us as an almost sacred text. There is an irony to this fact, as historian Pauline Maier has suggested (American Scripture: Making the Declaration of Independence, *New York: 1997). Jefferson and his congressional colleagues thought they were writing a secular, revolutionary document, not a work of eternal wisdom.*

"An Expression of the American Mind"

For the first decade or so after its writing, the Declaration of Independence was almost completely ignored; when considered at all, it was as a minor document. But during the 1790s, the Declaration re-emerged from oblivion and was often read aloud at Fourth of July celebrations. Jefferson was pleased and proud. In 1825, as his life neared its end, he offered this assessment of the Declaration's value in a letter to Henry Lee.

Source: Thomas Jefferson, *Writings*, ed. Merrill D. Peterson, New York: Library of America, 1984, p. 1501.

This was the object of the Declaration of Independence. Not to find out new principles, or new arguments, never before thought of, not merely to say things which had never been said before; but to place before mankind the common sense of the subject, in terms so plain and firm as to command their assent, and to justify ourselves in the independent stand we are compelled to take. Neither aiming at originality of principle or sentiment, nor yet copied from any particular and previous writing, it was intended to be an expression of the American mind, and to give to that expression the proper tone and spirit called for by the occasion. All its authority rests then on the harmonizing sentiments of the day, whether expressed in conversation, in letters, printed essays, or in the elementary books of public right, as Aristotle, Cicero, Locke, Sidney, &c.

This is the most famous copy of the Declaration and is popularly assumed to have been signed on July 4, 1776. In fact, this engrossed version was not available for signing until August 2, 1776. (Library of Congress)

IN CONGRESS, JULY 4, 1776.

A DECLARATION
BY THE REPRESENTATIVES OF THE
UNITED STATES OF AMERICA,
IN GENERAL CONGRESS ASSEMBLED.

WHEN in the Course of human Events, it becomes necessary for one People to dissolve the Political Bands which have connected them with another, and to assume among the Powers of the Earth, the separate and equal Station to which the Laws of Nature and of God entitle them, a decent Respect to the Opinions of Mankind requires that they should declare the causes which impel them to the Separation.

We hold these Truths to be self-evident, that all Men are created equal, that they are endowed by their Creator with certain unalienable Rights, that among these are Life, Liberty, and the Pursuit of Happiness—That to secure these Rights, Governments are instituted among Men, deriving their just Powers from the Consent of the Governed, that whenever any Form of Government becomes destructive of these Ends, it is the Right of the People to alter or to abolish it, and to institute new Government, laying its Foundation on such Principles, and organizing its Powers in such Form, as to them shall seem most likely to effect their Safety and Happiness. Prudence, indeed, will dictate that Governments long established should not be changed for light and transient Causes; and accordingly all Experience hath shewn, that Mankind are more disposed to suffer, while Evils are sufferable, than to right themselves by abolishing the Forms to which they are accustomed. But when a long Train of Abuses and Usurpations, pursuing invariably the same Object, evinces a Design to reduce them under absolute Despotism, it is their Right, it is their Duty, to throw off such Government, and to provide new Guards for their future Security. Such has been the patient Sufferance of these Colonies; and such is now the Necessity which constrains them to alter their former Systems of Government. The History of the present King of Great-Britain is a History of repeated Injuries and Usurpations, all having in direct Object the Establishment of an absolute Tyranny over these States. To prove this, let Facts be submitted to a candid World.

He has refused his Assent to Laws, the most wholesome and necessary for the public Good.

He has forbidden his Governors to pass Laws of immediate and pressing Importance, unless suspended in their Operation till his Assent should be obtained; and when so suspended, he has utterly neglected to attend to them.

He has refused to pass other Laws for the Accommodation of large Districts of People, unless those People would relinquish the Right of Representation in the Legislature, a Right inestimable to them, and formidable to Tyrants only.

He has called together Legislative Bodies at Places unusual, uncomfortable, and distant from the Depository of their public Records, for the sole Purpose of fatiguing them into Compliance with his Measures.

He has dissolved Representative Houses repeatedly, for opposing with manly Firmness his Invasions on the Rights of the People.

He has refused for a long Time, after such Dissolutions, to cause others to be elected; whereby the Legislative Powers, incapable of Annihilation, have returned to the People at large for their exercise; the State remaining in the mean time exposed to all the Dangers of Invasion from without, and Convulsions within.

He has endeavoured to prevent the Population of these States; for that Purpose obstructing the Laws for Naturalization of Foreigners; refusing to pass others to encourage their Migrations hither, and raising the Conditions of new Appropriations of Lands.

He has obstructed the Administration of Justice, by refusing his Assent to Laws for establishing Judiciary Powers.

He has made Judges dependent on his Will alone, for the Tenure of their Offices, and the Amount and Payment of their Salaries.

He has erected a Multitude of new Offices, and sent hither Swarms of Officers to harrass our People, and eat out their Substance.

He has kept among us, in Times of Peace, Standing Armies, without the consent of our Legislatures.

He has affected to render the Military independent of and superior to the Civil Power.

He has combined with others to subject us to a Jurisdiction foreign to our Constitution, and unacknowledged by our Laws; giving his Assent to their Acts of pretended Legislation:

For quartering large Bodies of Armed Troops among us:

For protecting them, by a mock Trial, from Punishment for any Murders which they should commit on the Inhabitants of these States:

For cutting off our Trade with all Parts of the World:

For imposing Taxes on us without our Consent:

For depriving us, in many Cases, of the Benefits of Trial by Jury:

For transporting us beyond Seas to be tried for pretended Offences:

For abolishing the free System of English Laws in a neighbouring Province, establishing therein an arbitrary Government, and enlarging its Boundaries, so as to render it at once an Example and fit Instrument for introducing the same absolute Rule into these Colonies:

For taking away our Charters, abolishing our most valuable Laws, and altering fundamentally the Forms of our Governments:

For suspending our own Legislatures, and declaring themselves invested with Power to legislate for us in all Cases whatsoever.

He has abdicated Government here, by declaring us out of his Protection and waging War against us.

He has plundered our Seas, ravaged our Coasts, burnt our Towns, and destroyed the Lives of our People.

He is, at this Time, transporting large Armies of foreign Mercenaries to compleat the Works of Death, Desolation, and Tyranny, already begun with circumstances of Cruelty and Perfidy, scarcely paralleled in the most barbarous Ages, and totally unworthy the Head of a civilized Nation.

He has constrained our fellow Citizens taken Captive on the high Seas to bear Arms against their Country, to become the Executioners of their Friends and Brethren, or to fall themselves by their Hands.

He has excited domestic Insurrections amongst us, and has endeavoured to bring on the Inhabitants of our Frontiers, the merciless Indian Savages, whose known Rule of Warfare, is an undistinguished Destruction, of all Ages, Sexes and Conditions.

In every stage of these Oppressions we have Petitioned for Redress in the most humble Terms: Our repeated Petitions have been answered only by repeated Injury. A Prince, whose Character is thus marked by every act which may define a Tyrant, is unfit to be the Ruler of a free People.

Nor have we been wanting in Attentions to our British Brethren. We have warned them from Time to Time of Attempts by their Legislature to extend an unwarrantable Jurisdiction over us. We have reminded them of the Circumstances of our Emigration and Settlement here. We have appealed to their native Justice and Magnanimity, and we have conjured them by the Ties of our common Kindred to disavow these Usurpations, which, would inevitably interrupt our Connections and Correspondence. They too have been deaf to the Voice of Justice and of Consanguinity. We must, therefore, acquiesce in the Necessity, which denounces our Separation, and hold them, as we hold the rest of Mankind, Enemies in War, in Peace, Friends.

We, therefore, the Representatives of the UNITED STATES OF AMERICA, in GENERAL CONGRESS, Assembled, appealing to the Supreme Judge of the World for the Rectitude of our Intentions, do, in the Name, and by Authority of the good People of these Colonies, solemnly Publish and Declare, That these United Colonies are, and of Right ought to be, FREE AND INDEPENDENT STATES; that they are absolved from all Allegiance to the British Crown, and that all political Connection between them and the State of Great-Britain, is and ought to be totally dissolved; and that as FREE AND INDEPENDENT STATES, they have full Power to levy War, conclude Peace, contract Alliances, establish Commerce, and to do all other Acts and Things which INDEPENDENT STATES may of right do. And for the support of this Declaration, with a firm Reliance on the Protection of divine Providence, we mutually pledge to each other our Lives, our Fortunes, and our sacred Honor.

Signed by ORDER and in BEHALF of the CONGRESS,

JOHN HANCOCK, PRESIDENT.

ATTEST.
CHARLES THOMSON, SECRETARY.

PHILADELPHIA: PRINTED BY JOHN DUNLAP.

Typeset by John Dunlap, this poster (or "broadside") edition of the Declaration first appeared on July 5, 1776. This copy is attached to the rough congressional journal. (Library of Congress)

A Declaration of Woman's Rights

As the Declaration grew in fame, it served as a revolutionary inspiration for people who remained excluded from America's hopes and dreams. The history-making Woman's Rights Convention of July, 1848 adopted its own version of the Declaration, drafted by Elizabeth Cady Stanton. Here are some excerpts from the first part of this document.

Source: Philip S. Foner, ed., *We, the Other People: Alternative Declarations of Independence by Labor Groups, Farmers, Woman's Rights Advocates, Socialists, and Blacks, 1829-1975*, Chicago: University of Illinois Press, 1976, pp. 78-81. (Foner's citation: Elizabeth Cady Stanton, Susan B. Anthony, and Matilda Joslyn Gage, eds., *History of Woman Suffrage*, Vol. 1, New York: 1881, pp. 70-4.) A longer excerpt from this is quoted in *Forward into Light: The Struggle for Woman's Suffrage* in the *Perspectives on History Series* from Discovery Enterprises, Ltd.

...We hold these truths to be self-evident: that all men and women are created equal; that they are endowed by their Creator with certain inalienable rights; that among these are life, liberty, and the pursuit of happiness; that to secure these rights governments are instituted, deriving their just powers from the consent of the governed....

The history of mankind is a history of repeated injuries and usurpations on the part of man toward woman, having in direct object the establishment of an absolute tyranny over her. To prove this, let facts be submitted to a candid world.

He has never permitted her to exercise her inalienable right to the elective franchise.

He has compelled her to submit to laws, in the formation of which she had no voice....

He has made her, if married, in the eye of the law, civilly dead....

After depriving her of all rights as a married woman, if single, and the owner of property, he has taxed her to support a government which recognizes her only when her property can be made profitable to it.

He has monopolized nearly all the profitable employments, and from those she is permitted to follow, she receives but a scanty remuneration. He closes against her all the avenues to wealth and distinction which he considers most honorable to himself....

He has denied her the facilities for obtaining a thorough education, all colleges being closed against her.

He allows her in Church, as well as State, but a subordinate position....

He has created a false public sentiment by giving to the world a different code of morals for men and women, by which moral delinquencies which exclude women from society, are not only tolerated, but deemed of little account in man....

He has endeavored, in every way that he could, to destroy her confidence in her own powers, to lessen her self-respect, and to make her willing to lead a dependent and abject life.

Now, in view of this entire disfranchisement of one-half the people of this country...we insist that they have immediate admission to all the rights and privileges which belong to them as citizens of the United States.

Abraham Lincoln's Declaration of Independence

According to some historians, the Declaration we read today can almost be said to have been authored by Abraham Lincoln. When, in his Gettysburg Address of 1863, Lincoln reminded his audience of our forefathers' "proposition that all men are created equal," he was putting the document to a use which many of its framers might not have predicted — the salvation of the Union and the abolition of slavery. This theme can be found much earlier in Lincoln's writings — for example, in the following passage from a speech he delivered in Springfield, Illinois on June 26, 1857.

Source: Abraham Lincoln, *Speeches and Writings: 1832-1858*, ed. Don E. Fehrenbacher, New York: Library of America, 1989, pp. 398-9.

I think the authors of that notable instrument intended to include *all* men, but they did not intend to declare all men equal *in all respects*. They did not mean to say all were equal in color, size, intellect, moral developments, or social capacity. They defined with tolerable distinctness, in what respects they did consider all men created equal — equal in "certain inalienable rights, among which are life, liberty, and the pursuit of happiness." This they said, and this meant. They did not mean to assert the obvious untruth, that all were then actually enjoying that equality, nor yet, that they were about to confer it immediately upon them. In fact they had no power to confer such a boon. They meant simply to declare the *right*, so that the *enforcement* of it might follow as fast as circumstances should permit. They meant to set up a standard maxim for free society, which should be familiar to all, and revered by all; constantly looked to, constantly labored for, and even though never perfectly attained, constantly approximated, and thereby constantly spreading and deepening its influence, and augmenting the happiness and value of life to all people of all colors everywhere. The assertion that "all men are created equal" was of no practical use in effecting our separation from Great Britain; and it was placed in the Declaration, not for that, but for future use. Its authors meant it to be, thank God, it is now proving itself, a stumbling block to those who in after times might seek to turn a free people back into the hateful paths of despotism. They knew the proneness of prosperity to breed tyrants, and they meant when such should re-appear in this fair land and commence their vocation they should find left for them at least one hard nut to crack.

Lincoln returned to this theme in the following passage from an 1859 letter to Henry L. Pierce. Note in Lincoln's invocation of "all men and all times" a contrast to Jefferson's own more modest evaluation of the Declaration as having expressed the "sentiments of the day."

Source: Abraham Lincoln, *Speeches and Writings: 1859-1865*, ed. Don E. Fehrenbacher, New York: Library of America, 1989, p. 19.

The principles of Jefferson are the definitions and axioms of free society. And yet they are denied and evaded, with no small show of success. One dashingly calls them "glittering generalities"; another bluntly calls them "self evident lies"; and still others insidiously argue that they apply only to "superior races."

These expressions, differing in form, are identical in object and effect — the supplanting the principles of free government, and restoring those of classification, caste, and legitimacy. They would delight a convocation of crowned heads, plotting against the people. They are the van-guard-the miners, and sappers — of returning despotism. We must repulse them, or they will subjugate us.

This is a world of compensations; and he who would *be* no slave, must consent to *have* no slave. Those who deny freedom to others, deserve it not for themselves; and, under a just God, can not long retain it.

All honor to Jefferson — to the man who, in the concrete pressure of a struggle for national independence by a single people, had the coolness, forecast, and capacity to introduce into a merely revolutionary document, an abstract truth, applicable to all men and all times, and so to embalm it there, that to-day, and in all coming days, it shall be a rebuke and a stumbling-block to the very harbingers of re-appearing tyranny and oppression.

A Black Declaration of Independence

Even before the Civil War, African Americans had found inspiration in the Declaration and its unfulfilled promise of equality. Black people have continued to invoke the Declaration during their struggle against white oppression, especially during the civil rights movement of the 1950s and 60s. In July, 1970, the National Committee of Black Churchmen issued a Black Declaration of Independence. Here are the opening paragraphs of this document.

Source: Philip S. Foner, ed., *op. cit.*, pp. 164-7. (Foner's citation: An advertisement in the *New York Times*, July 3, 1970.)

...When in the course of Human Events, it becomes necessary for a People who were stolen from the lands of their Fathers, transported under the most ruthless and brutal circumstances 5,000 miles to a strange land, sold into dehumanizing slavery, emasculated, subjugated, exploited and discriminated against for 351 years, to call, with finality, a halt to such indignities and genocidal practices — by virtue of the Laws of Nature and of Nature's God, a decent respect to the Opinions of Mankind requires that they should declare their just grievances and the urgent and necessary redress thereof.

We hold these truths to be self-evident, that all Men are not *only* created equal and endowed by their Creator with certain unalienable rights among which are Life, Liberty, and the Pursuit of Happiness, but that when this equality and these rights are deliberately and consistently refused, withheld or abnegated, men are bound by self-respect and honor to rise up in righteous indignation to secure them. Whenever any Form of Government, or any variety of established traditions and systems of the Majority becomes destructive of Freedom and of legitimate Human Rights, it is the Right of the Minorities to use every necessary and accessible means to protest and to disrupt the machinery of Oppression, and so to bring such general distress and discomfort upon the oppressor as to the offended Minorities shall seem most appropriate and most likely to effect a proper adjustment of the society.

...when a long train of Abuses, pursuing invariably the same Object, manifests a Design to reduce them under Absolute Racist Domination and Injustice, it is their Duty radically to confront such Government or system of traditions, and to provide, under the aegis of Legitimate Minority Power and Self Determination, for their present Relief and future Security. Such has been the patient Sufferance of Black People in the United States of America; and such is now the Necessity which constrains them to address this Declaration to Despotic White Power, and to give due notice of their determined refusal to be any longer silenced by fear or flattery, or to be denied justice. The history of the treatment of Black People in the United States is a history having in direct Object the Establishment and Maintenance of Racist Tyranny over this People. To prove this, let Facts be submitted to a candid World.

Epilogue:
An American Legend

What really happened during those first four fateful days of July, 1776? As the previous pages of this book suggest, the truth is somewhat at odds with popular legend. American independence was actually approved by Congress on July 2, not on July 4; the vote was twelve to zero, with New York abstaining. New York voted in favor of independence on July 7, finally making the decision unanimous. The adoption of the Declaration of Independence on July 4 was regarded by the delegates as little more than a legal formality — with important public relations implications, of course.

Perhaps most surprisingly, there is no evidence that a signing of the document took place on July 4. The only signatures put onto the document on that day seem to have been those of Congress' president John Hancock and its secretary Charles Thomson. The famous engrossed copy of the Declaration didn't become available for signing until August 2. Many of its famous signatures were not added until weeks or even months after that. Some of the signers had not been present in Congress on July 4, 1776 to vote on the Declaration's adoption, while some delegates who had been present on that day never became signers (Garry Wills, *Inventing America: Jefferson's Declaration of Independence*, New York: Doubleday, 1978, p. 339).

But the myth of a July 4 signing has proven very powerful — so powerful that Thomas Jefferson and John Adams both mistakenly came to believe that it had actually happened! Through good intentions and faulty memories, the two most important instigators of American independence generated more than their share of misinformation about the Declaration of Independence.

John Adams was correct, however, when he wrote to his wife Abigail on July 3, 1776, "It may be the Will of Heaven that America shall suffer

Calamities still more wasting and Distresses yet more dreadfull." The Revolutionary War would continue its destructive course until the United States defeated the British at Yorktown in 1781 with the help of the French fleet. Even after peace was declared in 1783, the new nation still faced the question of how to govern itself. The Federal Constitution, which went into effect in 1789, created a strong union but left the problem of slavery unsolved. It would take the tragic and terrible Civil War (1861-1865) to bring an end to slavery, but race relations in America remain deeply troubled to this day. Moreover, today's America faces the problem of maintaining unity in the face of vastly increasing cultural diversity. In a way, the War for American Independence still continues. With such a troubled history, perhaps we should be grateful for the benign mythology of our Declaration of Independence and its ennobling language.

The most magical story ever told about Thomas Jefferson and John Adams just happens to be true. On July 4, 1826, the fiftieth anniversary of their Declaration's adoption, both men were on their deathbeds. That morning, Jefferson awoke from a coma to ask his bedside companions, "Is it the Fourth?" He died shortly after noon. Adams passed away later the same day after murmuring these haunting last words:

"Thomas Jefferson survives."

Suggested Further Reading

Adams, Abigail and John Adams. *The Book of Abigail and John: Selected Letters of the Adams Family, 1762-1784.* Edited by L. H. Butterfield, Marc Friedlaender, and Mary-Jo Kline. Cambridge, MA: Harvard Press, 1975.

Bedini, Silvio A. *Declaration of Independence Desk: Relic of Revolution.* Washington: Smithsonian, 1981.

Beloff, Max, ed. The Debate on the American Revolution: 1761-1783. Dobbs Ferry, New York: Sheridan House, 1989.

Burke, Edmund. *Edmund Burke On the American Revolution.* Edited by Elliott R. Barkan. New York: Harper Torchbooks, 1966.

Chidsey, Donald Barr. *July 4, 1776: The Dramatic Story of the First Four Days of July, 1776.* New York: Crown, 1958.

Dudley, William, ed. *The American Revolution: Opposing Viewpoints®.* San Diego: Greenhven Press, 1992.

Foner, Philip S., ed. *We, the Other People: Alternative Declarations of Independence by Labor Groups, Farmers, Woman's Rights Advocates, Socialists, and Blacks, 1829-1975.* Chicago: University of Illinois Press, 1976.

Jefferson, Thomas. *The Life and Selected Writings of Thomas Jefferson.* Edited by Adrienne Koch and William Peden. New York: Random House, 1993.

—————. *The Papers of Thomas Jefferson.* Vol 1. Edited by Julian P. Boyd. Princeton: Princeton University Press, 1950.

—————. *Writings.* Edited by Merrill D. Peterson. New York: Library of America, 1984.

Maier, Pauline. *American Scripture: Making the Declaration of Independence.* New York: Knopf, 1997.

Munves, James. *Thomas Jefferson and the Declaration of Independence.* New York: Scribner's, 1978.

Paine, Thomas. *Rights of Man, Common Sense, and Other Political Writings.* Edited by Mark Philp, Oxford: Oxford University Press, 1995.

Wills, Garry. *Inventing America: Jefferson's Declaration of Independence.* New York: Doubleday, 1978.

Other References

Irving, Washington. The Complete Tales of Washington Irving, ed. Charles Neider. Garden City, New York: Doubleday, 1975.

Lincoln, Abraham. Speeches and Writings: 1832-1858. Edited by Don E. Fehrenbacher, New York: Library of America, 1989.

—————. Speeches and Writings: 1859-1865. Edited by Don E. Fehrenbacher, New York: Library of America, 1989.

Locke, John. An Essay Concerning Human Understanding. Edited by Peter H. Nidditch. Oxford: Clarendon, 1975.

—————. Second Treatise of Government. Edited by Richard H. Cox. Arlington Heights, Illinois: Harlan Davidson, 1982.

Randall, Henry S. The Life of Thomas Jefferson. 3 vols. New York: Derby & Jackson, 1858.

About the Editor

Wim Coleman is a freelance writer who lives in Chapel Hill, North Carolina. With his wife Pat Perrin, he has collaborated on two novels and a non-fiction book, as well as numerous works for educational publishers. *Terminal Games*, their suspense thriller about computer networking, was published by Bantam Books in 1994; foreign language editions have appeared in Japan, Germany, Italy, and Brazil.

Both Wim and Pat have edited and introduced several other titles for this *Perspectives on History Series*.